MW00715001

YOUR
30-DAY
JOURNEY
— T • O —
Kicking the Procrastination Habit

YOUR 30-DAY JOURNEY ~ T·O ~

Kicking the Procrastination Habit

Alyssa Haley

THOMAS NELSON PUBLISHERS
Nashville

Copyright © 1992 by Stephen Arterburn and Connie Neal

All rights reserved. Written permission must be secured from the publisher to use or reproduce any part of this book, except for brief quotations in critical reviews or articles.

Published in Nashville, Tennessee, by Oliver-Nelson Books, a division of Thomas Nelson, Inc., Publishers, and distributed in Canada by Lawson Falle, Ltd., Cambridge, Ontario.

The Bible version used in this publication is THE NEW KING JAMES VERSION. Copyright © 1979, 1980, 1982, Thomas Nelson, Inc., Publishers.

Printed in the United States.

Library of Congress Cataloging-in-Publication Data

Haley, Alyssa, 1958–
     Your 30-day journey to kicking the procrastination habit / Alyssa Haley.
          p.   cm.
     Includes bibliographical references.
     ISBN 0-8407-9642-0
     1. Procrastination. 2. Time management. I. Title. II. Title: Your thirty day journey to kick the procrastination habit.
BF637.P76H35   1992
155.2'32—dc20   92-32883
                                                          CIP

1 2 3 4 5 6 — 97 96 95 94 93 92

Contents

Introduction

This book is procrastinator friendly. Habitual procrastination can indicate many things . . . but not that you are hopelessly flawed! People procrastinate for many reasons. Your reasons probably make a lot of sense, if you consider what procrastination accomplishes for you. In these pages you will not find finger wagging, pep talks, or condemnation. You will find an easy, step-by-step way to reconsider your life and become more comfortable with yourself and more productive.

If you are thinking, "I'd like to read this book and take this journey . . . but I have to read all the other self-help books I've already bought," don't put this book down. By taking the manageable steps given in this journey, you will find tools to change your life. You might even actually get around to reading those other books.

Everyone has something on their mental "to do" list that keeps getting put off. You know you should do it. You feel a pang of guilt whenever you shuffle it to tomorrow's list. You realize you will have to do it eventually, although you secretly hope it will just disappear. You feel the weight of continually finding excuses . . . but you still procrastinate. Why?

Procrastination is often a puzzling problem. For some, it presents a mild irritation that occasionally interferes with life. For others, it can drastically affect productivity and significant relationships. When procrastination becomes habitual, you eventually pay a price for it. And yet, most people who procrastinate are not quite sure why they do it.

I will be your companion and guide for the journey, but you are in the driver's seat. You are in control of the process and are free to set your own pace. Although the book is arranged in thirty daily segments, there is no rule saying you have to complete the journey in thirty consecutive days. This is a journey you take for your own well-being.

You can kick the procrastination habit . . . and it doesn't have to be a chore. This journey can actually be fun! This can be a welcome season of refreshment if procrastination has developed into a puzzling habit that interferes with your goals or that robs you of joy.

You may see procrastination as a minor issue, or your habit may cause more substantial problems for you, resulting in lost jobs, opportunities, or relationships. To whatever degree habitual procrastination affects your life, you can kick the habit by considering what procrastination does *for* you and choosing more beneficial alternatives.

There are two kinds of books that deal with self-improvement topics: the kind that are helpful and encouraging and the kind which make you feel quite impressed with the author but quite guilty and inadequate as a person. The second type of book simply clutters your bookshelf and your already burdened conscience.

My sincere hope is that this book becomes a memento of experiences that helped you begin living life without undue procrastination. Years from now, when you find it tucked away behind a line of books or perhaps under a bed, may you feel no twinge of guilt for not having finished it, but may you smile with a sense of your own accomplishment.

You Don't Have to Do This!

Procrastination is often associated with things you feel you have to do, should do, or are expected to do. You may feel pulled between what you should do and what you want to do.

If you are going to find this journey useful, you must begin with the realization that you don't have to take this journey. It's your choice. Giving yourself the freedom *not* to take this journey will help take the pressure out of your decision.

Procrastination can also be associated with doubt about whether a decision or action is right or wrong. While you wrestle with the issue, time is slipping away.

You need to settle these doubts if you are going to enjoy taking this journey. Here is some help: Kicking the procrastination habit is a good thing to do for yourself any way you look at it.

You can clearly justify taking time for this journey by reminding yourself that the time you spend will be redeemed by making you better able to sort out the accumulation of pressing items on your mental "to do" list. Also, this journey is broken down into manageable portions designed to take no more than thirty minutes each day, not much time at all.

Another reason many procrastinate is because of fear of failure. You may fear that if you failed to reach a goal, you—as well as others—would see yourself as a failure. If you succeed, you fear you would be expected to succeed continually. For these reasons, you may hesitate to take steps to change your life, finding it less threatening to maintain the status quo.

During this journey there will be no grades given. You are not in competition, even with yourself. If you follow this journey, you will make some progress toward what you want to be able to accomplish in your life. On day thirty you will look back to see what you have accomplished and celebrate your progress. *Simply take each day as it comes and consider it an adventure toward a more productive life.*

PERSONAL EVALUATION

- What are ten things you do each day without hesitation?
- Do you agree that these things are not intimidating, are consistent with your values, and are things you want to do?

ACTION

Note something you procrastinate over in each of these four areas: it feels like an obligation, you are not sure it is O.K. to do, you think of other things that may be more important to do first, it involves a goal, and you fear finding out how you will measure up.

REFLECTION

Consider whether each of the things you do not procrastinate over fits the following description:

- Is it something you choose to do and/or want to do?
- Is it something you accept as being O.K. or right?
- Is it something that deserves your attention, even though there are other things you could spend your time on?
- Is it something that is not used to measure your worth or lack of worth, by yourself or others?

Think about the common denominators among the things you do not procrastinate over. What clues might that give you about why you procrastinate over certain things?

ENCOURAGEMENT

You don't have to complete this journey, but I hope you do because you have the opportunity to have more of what you want out of life if you choose to do this for yourself.

Procrastination Serves Your Purposes

As long as you view procrastination as something you can't control, you have no way of dealing with it. Once you realize that procrastination serves *your* purposes, it loses some of its mystery. *Understanding the benefits you receive from procrastinating gives you a fresh perspective that may become a key to unlock the door to a better way of life.*

You will not give up procrastination as a habit until you have found a more satisfying alternative that serves the same purpose. Once you identify the purpose(s) being served by procrastination, you will be in a much better position to eliminate the habit and replace it with a suitable alternative. In some instances you may decide that procrastination works to your advantage and elect to continue taking delayed action as a preferred response to specific circumstances.

PERSONAL EVALUATION

Here are some ways procrastination can serve specific purposes, even if you do not realize these motivating factors. Place a check next to any of these that describe how procrastinating has served you. You may also be able to think of others:

- Helps you sort out what is important to you
- Helps you avoid issues and situations that could prove painful, embarrassing, shameful, or difficult
- Allows you to avoid coming face-to-face with your human flaws
- Helps you remain in the comfort of the familiar, avoiding failure or the changes associated with possible success
- Is a useful way of communicating feelings (such as resentment, anger, disappointment, sadness) that you would never put into words
- Is a way of gaining power over someone in a position of power over you
- Allows you to get out of doing something you didn't want to do
- Provides you with a buffer between yourself and discovering the best of your ability
- Allows you to make promises with the chance of not having to follow through
- Keeps you from being overwhelmed
- Keeps you from making a wrong decision by making no decision
- Gives you enjoyment you feel you are being deprived of in your daily commitments
- Protects you from facing activities and situations that trigger unresolved emotional issues
- Gives you a high feeling when you put things off then rush to achieve whatever is required, just in the nick of time

If you benefit from procrastination in other ways add those ways to the list.

ACTION

For each item you checked, cite one example from your own life of what you procrastinated over and how it served that particular purpose. For example: If you checked that procrastination allowed you to get out of doing something you didn't want to do, your example might be that as a child your mother would do your chores if you put them off long enough.

REFLECTION

You are probably accustomed to thinking of procrastination as a problem. For the moment, consider how procrastination has been a useful tool. In each of the experiences you cited above, consider the problems or difficulties you *avoided* (if only momentarily) when you procrastinated.

ENCOURAGEMENT

Taking a fresh point of view in dealing with a persistent problem can yield fresh insights and solutions. Allow yourself to look at procrastination in a new way.

FOOD FOR THOUGHT

He that lies upon the ground cannot fall.
                                        —Yiddish Proverb

Kicking the Habit Means Learning to Choose

Kicking the procrastination habit means learning to choose what you want to put off until later and learning to make choices which enable you to do the things you need to do. Daily life requires making choices, moment by moment, of what you will do now, postpone until later, or not do at all.

Here are some choices that can help you kick the procrastination habit.

Choose to Expect Less of Yourself in a Given Time Frame.

If you consistently schedule too little time to accomplish your tasks, you will repeatedly have to put things off or get time extensions. In this way, you set yourself up to look like a procrastinator. By choosing to lower your expectations or by giving yourself more time to reach your self-imposed goals, you will reduce the need to put off other routine commitments.

Choose to Decide How You Want to Live Your Life.

Procrastination seems to be a problem only when you put off things that conflict with your stated commitments and values. Maybe the real problem is that the values you espouse are not really your own. Therefore, when it comes to carrying through on the work involved, you lack the internal motivation. You may be trying to live to please someone else or to fulfill their dreams for you. For example: Let's say your parents always wanted you to become a doctor, and they sacrificed their resources to put you through medical school. You, however, discover that the field of medicine holds little interest for you. You may go along with their dreams for you on a superficial level, but you may experience an inner resistance to doing the work involved in completing medical training. You may find yourself chronically procrastinating on your studies.

You have a right to choose what you do with your life. You have the right to choose what priorities are important to you and to make your time management decisions on that basis. You are also the one who will live with the consequences of your decisions. This takes courage and may even require some form of support to deal with the reactions of those you had previously been living to please.

Choose to Trade, Delegate, and Dump Some Duties.

If you dislike taking out the garbage, negotiate with others in your family to trade duties. Ask them what chore they dislike and see if you can make a trade with someone who is not as reluctant to take out the trash. You can also choose to delegate the tasks you really don't want to do.

Choose to Hire Someone to Do the Things You Keep Putting Off.

There are services available to do almost anything you can think of—including cleaning out your garage, handling your taxes, reorganizing your closet, or grocery shopping. If costs are prohibitive, consider using the services of neighborhood teens or bartering services.

Choose to Redefine Commitments More Realistically.

If you have promised to do things that you are now putting off because you have overcommitted your time, energy, or money, you can choose to redefine those commitments. This may mean sincerely apologizing for making a promise you cannot keep at this season of your life or rescheduling your commitment for a realistic time in the future.

Choose to Lower the Stakes.

If you tell yourself a task must be perfect, if your self-esteem is at stake, you will hesitate to begin or you will have a hard time knowing when enough is enough. You may focus so much time and attention on one task that others have to be postponed.

You have the ability to choose to redefine what something means to your life. When you learn to lower the stakes in your own mind, you will be less intimidated and more apt to get on with the job. For example: If you dream of being a renowned novelist and find yourself paralyzed in your attempts to complete your first novel, it may be because you have told yourself that your first novel will determine your reputation. You may think that if it doesn't hit the *New York Times* best-sellers list, your hopes of literary success are finished. Is it any wonder you would hesitate to start each chapter and never feel the work was ready? You could help yourself overcome procrastination by lowering the stakes. You could make your aim to complete three publishable works of fiction, before writing your fourth novel from which you would expect great things. To lower the stakes you need not lower your standards of excellence. You can still do your very best, but without the added pressure that may make it impossible to accomplish anything.

PERSONAL EVALUATION

- For each of the choices above, identify one area where you procrastinate that might be helped by making that kind of choice. (You don't have to commit to change, just identify the possibility.)
- How would your choices be lived out if you were to put them into action?

ACTION

Select the one choice you feel most comfortable with. Clearly define the action prompted by the choice you have made, and practice doing those things.

FOOD FOR THOUGHT

All changes, even the most longed for, have their melancholy; for what we leave behind us is a part of ourselves; we must die to one life before we can enter into another.

—Anatole France

Finding Motivation, Envisioning Your Rewards

To achieve any goal, you must first be able to envision the benefits of achieving that goal. Kicking the procrastination habit is actually a non-goal in the sense that you are aiming to stop *not* doing things. To envision the benefits of *not* procrastinating, you need to envision how you will feel when you don't put things off.

Don't start this journey by heaping guilt on yourself. Try a more positive approach.

- Focus on what is in it for you. Initially, forget all others affected by your procrastination and ask yourself, "How would kicking the procrastination habit help me feel better about me and my life?"
- Envision yourself handling matters promptly in areas where you have previously procrastinated. Imagine the sense of self-respect you will feel and the relief from guilt.
- Envision yourself being relieved of the negative consequences that have resulted from chronic procrastination. Henry David Thoreau's comment, "As if you could kill time without injuring eternity," illustrates that procrastination does have the power to destroy the fiber of your life. Envision being spared negatives like a routine fight between you and your spouse because you are always late.

- Envision how each area of your life would be enhanced if you were able to manage your time without hesitation and fear. Consider how procrastination impacts each area of life: career, family, finances, personal life, emotional life, spiritual life, friendships, health, and so on. *Now imagine how each area of your life would be improved if procrastination were not a problem for you.*

PERSONAL EVALUATION

- In what ways would you feel better about yourself and your life if you were able to kick the procrastination habit?
- What matters would you now be able to face without hesitation? How would this benefit you?
- What negative consequences of procrastinating would you avoid?
- How would each area of life (career, family, finances, personal life, emotional life, spiritual life, friendships, and health) be improved if you were able to kick the procrastination habit?

REFLECTION

Take some time to envision each of the items you thought about during the personal evaluation. Try to imagine each scene in full color, complete with positive comments from others, feelings of accomplishment and self-satisfaction, and the new positive consequences that would result from kicking the procrastination habit.

FOOD FOR THOUGHT

Believe that life is worth living and your belief will help you create the fact.

—William James

Give Yourself Some Slack

People who tend to procrastinate are often perfectionists. If you measure your self-esteem by how well you produce or perform, it is no wonder that the important things in life—the things you value most—seem to be the most difficult to face.

You can help yourself kick the procrastination habit by giving yourself some slack. Here are some specific ways you can do so:

Consider Whether Perfectionism Is an Issue You Need to Redefine.

No one is perfect. If you hold to standards of perfection which are unrealistically demanding, take time to challenge the assumptions you have accepted. Seriously contemplate why you feel you must be perfect. When you get to the bottom of the issues, you will be able to give yourself some slack.

Understand and Accept Your Personality and Personal Style.

Try not to compare yourself with others and expect to perform as they do. You have your own unique personality. While some personality types find it easy to meticulously attend to details and follow one project through to completion before making another commitment, other personality types tend to become interested in many things and are easily distracted. In Florence Littauer's books

Personality Plus and *The Personality Puzzle* you can find detailed descriptions of various personality types and their unique life-styles. *If you learn to accept your personality, you can learn to be more tolerant of yourself.*

Understand and Accept Your Internal Time Clock.

If you are a night person who has bursts of creativity in the evening hours, don't condemn yourself when you can't get going in the morning. Instead accept your unique rhythms and try to set up your work schedule to make the most of the times when you are at your best.

PERSONAL EVALUATION

- Do you judge your value on the basis of who you are or on how you perform?
- Might you be a perfectionist? If so, is this something you pride yourself on, or do you see that your perfectionism could be a symptom of a problem?
- Do you understand how your unique personality type relates to your tendency to procrastinate?
- Are you willing to take your body clock into consideration and place fewer demands on yourself when you are not at peak performance?

ACTION

If perfectionism is a dominant part of your life, get a book or speak with a counselor about the possible implications of perfectionism.

Read a book dealing with various personality types and gather enough information to help you learn to appreciate your strengths.

Consider whether you could change your schedule in some way to make the most of your best times and give yourself some slack when you are tired.

REFLECTION

Think about how giving yourself some slack in the ways mentioned above could change your attitude about the things you tend to procrastinate over.

ENCOURAGEMENT

Everyone deserves some slack. If you have been unwilling to give yourself this gift, you can change that today.

FOOD FOR THOUGHT

There is a difference between
striving for excellence,
and striving for perfection.
The first is attainable, gratifying
and healthy.
The second is unattainable,
frustrating and neurotic.
It is also a terrible waste of time.

—Edwin Bliss

Neglect, Avoidance, or Refusal?

There are varying degrees of procrastination and various underlying issues which create the need to procrastinate. If you can discover what is behind your tendency to procrastinate in a particular area, you will have a much better chance of coming up with an appropriate response. I have divided procrastination patterns into three general categories: those things you simply neglect to do, those things you avoid, those things you refuse to take responsibility for.

Items you neglect are those which you never seem to have time to do. You don't care enough to follow through, but you may still believe that you should do these things. This category can indicate your true priorities and values.

The most notable difference between the neglect and avoidance categories is the emotional intensity. Whereas you may neglect things without registering any feeling, the things you avoid are usually associated with feelings of fear, pain, sadness, or other unpleasant emotions.

The final category is refusal to deal with something. Although you may not have made a conscious decision, you have determined that you *will not* deal with certain aspects of life, nor accept responsibility for particular tasks. *Procrastination by refusal is often part of a power struggle.* A teenage child who has been told to clean his room may respond with "I will later." He may really be refusing parental control. He may also use his stalling tactics to see just how far he can go without experiencing negative consequences.

PERSONAL EVALUATION

· What things do you neglect doing, although you believe you should do them?
· What things do you avoid doing because they stir up unpleasant emotions?
· What things do you refuse to accept responsibility for? Why do you think you procrastinate rather than clearly stating your refusal?

ACTION

Divide a sheet of paper into three columns. Label these: Neglect, Avoidance, and Refusal. Quickly try to list as many things as you can which fall into each category. Don't take a lot of time, just note each idea in the category which seems to fit the closest.

REFLECTION

The things you neglect may reveal what you actually believe to be unworthy of your time and effort. The things you avoid may give clues about areas of life where you have been wounded. The things you refuse to do can point out some of the relationships where you are actively involved in a power struggle. Consider each of these areas, looking for a deeper understanding of underlying issues. Later, you may want to explore your insights from a broader perspective.

ENCOURAGEMENT

When you dare to go beyond dealing with the symptoms to deal with underlying causes, you may gain a great deal more from your journey than just kicking the habit of procrastination. Dare to look deeper!

FOOD FOR THOUGHT

People will allow their faults to be shown them; they will let themselves be punished for them; they will patiently endure many things because of them; they only become impatient when they have to learn to lay them aside.

—Goethe

Minor Details: It Is Just Not That Important!

In our fast-paced, complex, technologically sophisticated society there is an overload of information and options. You have responsibilities related to each role you play: employer, parent, child, family member, church member, citizen, and so on. You are confronted with political issues on a local, state, national, and international level. You are faced with needs from all over the globe, from children starving in the third world to environmental issues which are reported to threaten the continued existence of the planet. For each problem there is someone telling you that you should care and do something to combat these problems. You are bombarded with requests for charitable donations on a local level as well—many of which seem worthy of your support.

You simply can't respond to everything you are told you should care about. *Streamlining is in! You can choose to simplify your life* in these ways:

Identify What Is of Minor Importance in This Season of Your Life.

If you are raising small children, you may decide that—for this season—you are not going to focus on maintaining a demanding social calendar. If you are busy building your career, you may decide that personally maintaining your lawn just doesn't rate high enough for you to do it yourself.

Take Obligations Off Your Mental List.

When you determine that something is of minor importance to you at this time, you are not saying that those things have no value. If you still have a sense of obligation to something on your list of minor importance, consider giving of your resources instead of your time.

Find More Efficient Ways to Accomplish Things Which Are Important or Necessary Parts of Life.

If cooking nutritious, homemade meals for your family is important to you, you may be able to find ways to accomplish this goal in a shorter amount of time. For example: Tupperware has designed a stack cooker for the microwave oven where you can cook your entire meal within twenty-five minutes. By making similar discoveries and changing your everyday routine, you can save more time to use in other ways.

Get Rid of Possessions Which Require Too Much Upkeep.

For example, one couple found that the expansive home they had treasured while raising their five children had become a burden to them after the last of their children went off to college. When they moved to a condominium, they spent less time procrastinating and more time playing golf and enjoying one another's company.

PERSONAL EVALUATION

- What are some things that seem of minor importance to you during this season of life, which you nevertheless have felt obligated to continue?
- Are you willing to give yourself permission to remove some of these from your mental list of obligations?
- What are some things you do as a part of your routine that you could do more efficiently?
- What possessions do you have which may not be worth the amount of time they require?

ACTION

Make some specific change in your life that will relieve you of some of the minor details in your routine.

ENCOURAGEMENT

You can choose to enjoy a simplified life. Do yourself the favor of paring your life down to doing those things which truly matter to you.

FOOD FOR THOUGHT

There cannot be a crisis next week. My schedule is already full.

—Henry Kissinger

Confused or Conflicting Priorities

If your priorities are confused, you will continually struggle with procrastination. When you are not certain what is important to you, you will lack guidelines which allow you to put things off with a clear conscience. You will always have the sense that you are probably not spending your time in the right way, but you will never feel sure.

An example of procrastination resulting from confused priorities would be someone who works out of an office in the home. If that person has never clearly defined work hours as separate from household duties, they may find themselves putting in a load of laundry, running errands, answering phone calls from friends, helping the kids with homework, and so on. All of these things are important, but by failing to clarify the order of importance *during work hours* the person has a problem with procrastination.

Having conflicting priorities is more than just being uncertain about what is important to you. Things that are important to you may be in competition with one another. An example of conflicting priorities is wanting to be the best parent you can be —spending not only quality time but a quantity of time with your children—and also wanting to become CEO (chief executive officer) of your corporation.

The number 1 *New York Times* best-seller, *A Passion For Excellence* by Tom Peters and Nancy Austin points out that the belief that you can have it all and simultaneously be the best at it all is simply not true. The authors say,

> We are frequently asked if it is possible to "have it all"—a full and satisfying personal life and a full and satisfying, hard-working, professional one. Our answer is: No. The price of excellence is time, energy, attention, and focus, at the very same time that energy, attention, and focus could have gone toward enjoying your daughter's soccer game. Excellence is a high cost item. As David Ogilvy observed in *Confessions of an Advertising Man:* "If you prefer to spend all your spare time growing roses or playing with your children, I like you better, but do not complain that you are not being promoted fast enough."

If you hold excellence up as your crowning virtue, you may be at a deadlock in areas where your priorities conflict. The only way to alleviate the procrastination resulting from this kind of internal deadlock is to *finish the fight within you and allow one side to win.*

PERSONAL EVALUATION

- When are you confused over whether there is something more important to do than what you are doing? Think back over the past week and cite a specific example.

- What do you value in life? Include things such as: family relationships, your marriage, cultivating friendships, dating, parenting, work, hobbies, political involvement, civic involvement, education, recreation, spirituality, physical fitness, and creating and managing your home.
- When do you experience a conflict between priorities that you value? How does this relate to your tendency to procrastinate?

ACTION

List everything you value as being worthy of your time and attention on some level.

Place a check next to each item if you can recall a time when you experienced confusion over whether you should be doing that task or another important task.

Place a star next to each item if you tend to procrastinate before you get started. Note what you think to yourself while you are procrastinating. Take special note if you are thinking that you should be doing something else but you are confused about which to do first.

Circle any items which seem to be in conflict, and draw a line connecting the two circles.

REFLECTION

Do you use your time to do things you really value? If not, is it because of economic necessity? Are you adapting your life to please someone else? What can you do to plan for a future where you will be better able to spend your time on things you value?

ENCOURAGEMENT

By identifying where confusion and conflict exist, you are paving the way to greater productivity and peace of mind. Don't hold back. Every point of confusion and conflict you identify can be dealt with.

FOOD FOR THOUGHT

To everything there is a season,
A time for every purpose under heaven.
>   —From *Ecclesiastes*

Time Out: Overcommitted and Undernourished

If your life is filled with things you have to do, are expected to do, should do, and ought to do—without much of what you enjoy, procrastination may be your only way to find time for you. The man who is overworked and overtired may justify putting off an important project to play video games on his computer, saying "I need a break." Yet he cannot enjoy the break he truly needs because he has procrastinated to get the break.

Every human being needs time to nourish body, mind, and spirit. For some reason, this doesn't seem to come naturally. If it did, God probably wouldn't have had to command the human race to take one day each week to rest from work, to refresh themselves and to renew their relationship with God. Just as nature shows you there are times to grow, to decline, to wake, and sleep, you need to find a balance in life that allows for physical, emotional, mental, and spiritual ebb and flow.

PERSONAL EVALUATION

- Can you think of times when you procrastinate in order to give yourself a much needed break?
- What time do you set aside each week to do things which nourish you physically, emotionally, mentally, and spiritually?

• If you were able to set aside all of today's demands, what would you say you *need* to do for your own well-being?

ACTION

List the needs you have identified as necessary for your well-being.

For each area of life where you are feeling undernourished, list something you could do that would nourish you.

REFLECTION

Imagine how your life could be better one year from now if you would guard some time each day and one day each week to nourish yourself.

ENCOURAGEMENT

You may hesitate to devote time to yourself when you could be using it to "get ahead." You will find that if you take time to nourish yourself, you will become more productive in the time you do work.

FOOD FOR THOUGHT

Remember the Sabbath day, to keep it holy. Six days you shall labor and do all your work, but the seventh day is the Sabbath of the Lord your God. For in six days the Lord made the heavens and the earth, the sea, and all that is in them, and rested the seventh day. Therefore the Lord blessed the Sabbath day and hallowed it.

—From the Ten Commandments

Please . . . No Pain

No one wants to hurt. Whenever you have enough knowledge and experience to realize that something will hurt—even if you know it is necessary for your ultimate health—you will probably be inclined to procrastinate. People avoid physical pain by postponing visits to the dentist or necessary surgery. People who have experienced severe sexual, physical, or emotional trauma are known to postpone the emotional pain of dealing with what happened to them by completely blocking the awareness of the experience from their consciousness.

Putting things off may be your way to avoid getting too close to your emotional pain. Examining areas where you procrastinate when you don't understand why may lead you to discover areas of personal injury that truly need attention and healing. Not everything you procrastinate about hides a wound. However, if the reason for procrastination is a mystery, there is a good chance that it may be a means of avoiding the threat of pain.

You desire to overcome procrastination, but you may not be interested in groping around for underlying causes. In fact, if there are some hidden emotional injuries in your life, you will probably recoil at the thought of poking around where it might hurt. However, once the deeper issue is dealt with, there will be no reason for you to continue procrastinating in this area.

PERSONAL EVALUATION

- What do you procrastinate over because you are hesitant to deal with the pain involved?
- Are you putting off something right now because you fear it will hurt?
- Are there some things you procrastinate over which are a mystery to you, where you experience a vague uneasiness or irrational resistance when you think about doing them?

ACTION

Begin to prepare yourself emotionally to face your fears and hurts later in the journey and to find alternative ways of dealing with the possible pain. Then you will be able to choose whether procrastination is your best choice.

REFLECTION

Take some time to think about how you feel about facing your fears. Notice which areas cause you the most concern. If you gain insight into what you may be afraid of and why, note these things for your own information.

ENCOURAGEMENT

You are perfectly normal in your desire to avoid pain, although life includes pain for everyone. Summon the courage and realism you will need to deal appropriately with the pain in your life.

FOOD FOR THOUGHT

No pain, no gain.

Avoiding Embarrassment and Shame

Embarrassment and shame are similar, yet different. For the purpose of our journey, let's define embarrassment as an uncomfortable feeling associated with something you do that is socially unacceptable. Shame is also an uncomfortable emotion, but the distinction is that shame is associated with some socially unacceptable flaw in who you are—not just what you do. Embarrassment occurs when you make a mistake. Shame occurs when you believe you *are* a mistake, and you fear that someone may discover the awful truth about you and reject or ridicule you. Both the desire to avoid embarrassment and the need to cover unhealthy internal shame have power to trigger procrastination.

An example of procrastinating to avoid embarrassment would be a woman who is illiterate procrastinating over looking for employment. The thought of being asked to fill out a standard application form is intimidating, even if she has the qualifications to perform the job.

An example of procrastination associated with internalized shame would be a child who lives in a family where he is continually criticized. This child may procrastinate over going to school or taking tests, for fear that the teacher will discover that he really is an idiot. The shame can prompt him to protect himself by putting off doing anything which will measure his intelligence and possibly prove his parents correct.

PERSONAL EVALUATION

- What experiences can you recall where you were embarrassed? Can you think of subsequent situations where you procrastinated in an attempt to avoid being embarrassed like that again?
- What is there about you that you fear may be flawed?
- Where did your feelings of being flawed or inadequate originate? Who pointed out that there was something wrong with you? Have you ever challenged those shameful assumptions?
- What do you procrastinate over that may be associated with the shameful belief that someone may discover your secret flaws?
- Are there certain kinds of relationships that intimidate you? Are your relationships possibly hindered because of procrastination born out of internalized shame?

ACTION

List anything you put off or procrastinate over which may be related to wanting to avoid embarrassment or shame.

List the things you see as being flawed about you that you would never want anyone to find out. For each thing you notice as being a source of shame for you, identify anything you procrastinate over that is related.

Identify and list any shame-causing life experiences that convince you of your flaws. Later in your journey you will have some help dealing with these issues. For the next few days, think about what might be contributing to the shame you feel.

REFLECTION

Just like the little boy who was verbally abused in the example above, you may believe shameful things about yourself which may not be true. If you continue to procrastinate to cover your shame, you may miss the opportunity to expose the lies about yourself that you have been led to believe. Think about the possibility of discovering you are not as bad as you assume.

ENCOURAGEMENT

Courageously considering issues which are embarrassing or shameful can lead to finding ways to resolve the shame and rid yourself of one cause of chronic procrastination.

FOOD FOR THOUGHT

Then the eyes of both of them were opened, and they knew that they were naked; and they sewed fig leaves together and made themselves coverings. . . . Then the LORD God called to Adam and said to him, "Where are you?" So he said, "I heard

Your voice in the garden, and I was afraid because I was naked; and I hid myself."

—Genesis 3:7, 9–11

You are only as sick as the secrets you keep.

—Alcoholics Anonymous Slogan

Fear of Failure, Fear of Success

Fear of failure and fear of success are two of the most common causes of procrastination. *Any time you undertake a task, you risk both failure and success*—each of which may be accompanied by potential problems. If you do fear the risk involved in having your work or creativity measured, you may find life more comfortable if you procrastinate whenever faced with such a risk.

Here are some perceived risks you may associate with the possibility of failure:

If your work is used as a measure of your worth, to fail at something will damage your self-esteem. Some people are secure in their inherent worth as human beings and accept occasional failure as a normal part of the human condition. Other people do not accept themselves as valuable, unless they are continually doing something to prove their worth. John Bradshaw calls this "a human doing rather than a human being."

If you are being judged by others who have power over your quality of life, doing something with measurable results can cause great fear. For example, if your boss says she is watching you to judge if you are performing your job up to company standards, it is understandable that you might hesitate at any project which could be used to determine whether you get to keep your job.

If you are trying to please someone with your performance, you may balk at efforts which would measure how well you compare to their ideal of you. For example, if your dad always dreamed of you being the all-star quarterback in college, you may procrastinate in trying out for the team because this test will determine whether you are able to please your father. Conversely, you may also hesitate at tests that give you the opportunity to prove someone wrong about you when they said you couldn't do something worthwhile. Suppose one of your teachers told you that you didn't have what it took to make it in law school, but you persisted, energized by your determination to prove them wrong. You might be inclined to procrastinate when facing your bar exam because of the internalized fear that your failure would prove them right about your limitations.

Here are some perceived risks you may associate with the fear of success:

If you succeed there is the risk that others may resent your success and stop associating with you in a positive way. Single women may fear that great financial success may intimidate potential suitors. Married women may fear that if their success exceeds that of their husbands, it will lead to marital difficulties. Men who become highly successful may fear that they will no longer fit in the group of guys they grew up with. Some family members resent and ridicule success that sets one sibling in a higher social standing than others.

If you succeed you may not be sure whether people who claim to love you and care about you are sincere, or merely want to be associated with someone successful.

If you succeed and ascend to a higher position in your work, you may fear that more will be expected of you until you become overwhelmed.

If you succeed your life-style would change, and you may fear leaving your current situation where you feel confident and comfortable.

PERSONAL EVALUATION

- When do you experience fear of failure? Why?
- If you fail at something, what conclusions does that cause you to draw about yourself?
- How is fear of failure associated with your procrastination habit?
- In what endeavors do you experience a fear of success? Why?
- In what specific ways do you procrastinate to keep yourself from experiencing the success you could achieve if you gave your best performance?

ACTION

List anything you procrastinate over because of a fear of failure. For each item, list all the negative consequences which you suppose would happen if you were to fail at that particular task.

List anything you procrastinate over because of a fear of success. For each item, list all the negative consequences which you suppose would happen if you were to succeed at that particular task.

REFLECTION

Choose one item from your fear of failure and one item from your fear of success list. Try to imagine some way you could live comfortably with yourself if you were to fail or succeed in each area. For example: Imagine failing a test and having your teacher offer to help you learn the concepts you don't understand. Imagine being given a promotion and your friends congratulating you.

FOOD FOR THOUGHT

What we must decide is perhaps how we are valuable rather than how valuable we are.

—Edgar Z. Friedenberg

Monsters in the Dark: Fear of the Unknown

Remember how childhood fears of monsters in the dark could paralyze you and keep you from getting a needed drink of water? *Fear of the unknown may still paralyze some people,* keeping them from moving ahead on even simple tasks.

Six months ago Sandra's toddler used her car tape deck as a piggy bank, inserting a handful of change into the slot where the tapes belong. Sandra misses being able to play tapes, but she still hasn't gotten around to getting it repaired. She doesn't know where to take it or how much it will cost.

Kathy hasn't balanced her checkbook in three months, and she dreads the thought of doing so. She doesn't know how much money she has, how much she has gone over her budget, or how long it will take to straighten out her accounts since she let them go.

Gerald inherited a substantial sum of money when his father passed away two years ago. He keeps it in a secure savings account that yields a low rate of return. He keeps planning to decide on more profitable investments, but doesn't have the confidence or financial knowledge. He doesn't know whom he can trust as a dependable financial advisor. These people are procrastinating because of something unknown that keeps them from moving forward.

A radio commercial for a seminar on how to live up to your potential told a story of a farmer who mowed around a large flat stone in his field. Each year he fretted over the added work involved in having to carefully maneuver around the stone that kept him from using his entire field for crops. He assumed, from the breadth of the stone, that it went down deep into the earth—so he procrastinated. After years of putting off the task, he finally got out the backhoe and tried to move the stone. It moved easily. He could have moved the one-inch-thick stone by hand. Yet, he had limited his productivity because he hesitated to confront the unknown "monster."

Sometimes you may put off attempting something—like a minor repair or a financial investment—because you assume that it will be a major undertaking. You may become overwhelmed with your assumption while the true level of difficulty remains a mystery.

PERSONAL EVALUATION

- What do you put off that is on your mental list of things to do, or things you want to do, because of some unknown factor which intimidates you?

ACTION

Identify five things that you put off because of the unknown.

For each item, list everything you need to know before you could complete these things.

ENCOURAGEMENT

In many cases you will discover, like the farmer moving the stone, that gaining information about the situation will lead to a simple way to accomplish tasks which at first seem overwhelming or intimidating. Dare to try to lift the stones in your way.

FOOD FOR THOUGHT

We should not let our fears hold us back from pursuing our hopes.

—John F. Kennedy

The Silent Power of Procrastination

When procrastination is used in a power struggle it can be a very useful tool, perhaps even a weapon. *In situations where you lack overt power, you may find considerable power in procrastinating.*

Here are some examples: A child may take his time in complying with a parent's command in an attempt to convey his independence and perhaps his anger.

In the cartoon series "The Jetsons," George Jetson feigns submission to his tyrannical boss, Mr. Spacely, while continuing a pattern of being late for work and taking his time in doing his job.

Donna was aware that her new mother-in-law was trying to manipulate her into sending greeting cards to her husband's side of the family for every holiday on the calendar. Instead of confronting the issue verbally, Donna simply waited and mailed even the cards she regularly sent a short time after the occasion had passed. Procrastination was her silent way of stating that she refused to be overpowered or manipulated.

When a husband or wife is being required to do something, they may put it off while smiling and promising to get around to the unwelcome task. "Yes, Dear, I'll get to that soon" may really mean "I will get around to it when I choose or when you show me enough respect to ask instead of demand."

An administrative assistant was asked to type a document she found laborious. It was not the kind of work she had agreed to in her job description. She felt typing was beneath her position and was peeved that she had to do it. She dared not admit this to her boss, however, for fear she might lose her job. Instead she typed the majority of the report but put off completing the footnotes. By putting this off she gained a sense of power, since she knew her boss could not turn in the report until the footnotes were complete.

In the political arena, labor strikes are a very effective way to use procrastination as a bargaining chip. When labor unions decide to put off going to work, they are using a form of procrastination to exert their power.

PERSONAL EVALUATION

- In what ways does procrastination give you a sense of power in situations where someone has power over you?
- When have you used the silent power of procrastination to convey a message or emotional statement which you were unwilling to state verbally?
- What results did you achieve?
- Does using procrastination as a means of exerting your power have negative consequences for you?

REFLECTION

Think about a time when procrastination worked to your advantage in a power struggle. How did you feel? Now try to think of a time when procrastination backfired and hurt you when you tried to use it in a power struggle.

ENCOURAGEMENT

Don't be afraid to use procrastination to help you in a power struggle if it will serve your purpose and is your best alternative. However, make sure that your choice of procrastination instead of more direct means of communication doesn't hurt you and others.

Promising to Please: Thinking "No" but Saying "Yes"

If you have the tendency to say yes at times when you really wish you could say no, you are setting yourself up to procrastinate. If you gain the reputation of someone people can turn to whenever they need help, you will be frequently asked for assistance. A time will come when you will be overcommitted. Then you will either procrastinate in the area of your promises or in other areas so you have time to fulfill your many commitments. You may also experience an undercurrent of resentment toward those who have asked for your help. If so, you will lack the internal motivation to follow through promptly with your commitment.

There are many reasons people develop the habit of saying yes when they want to say no.

You Fear the Person's Reaction.

In the movie *The Godfather*, whenever someone agreed to do what the Mafia "asked," the mobsters explained their cooperation by saying, "I made him an offer he couldn't refuse." Their meaning, of course, was that if the person had refused it would have cost him dearly—probably his life. There are times someone asks you to do something and you realize that saying no may have grave consequences

59

You Feel It Is Part of Your Role to Say Yes.

Some families feel that to say no to a request is tantamount to saying that you don't love the person. Phrases like, "How can I refuse my own mother?" reflect the kind of familial relationships which lock family members into responses that don't allow for honesty or even a healthy maintenance of personal boundaries.

You Want to Be Seen in a Positive Light.

Some people cannot resist volunteering for every unwanted position or task up for grabs. *If you are ceaselessly trying to please in every group, you quickly become overcommitted and have to procrastinate* and juggle commitments.

You Fear Rejection.

You may say yes out of your fear that the only way you can stay in everyone's good graces is to do what they want at all times. If this describes you, the time will come when you grow to resent the imbalance of this type of relationship. However, those to whom you say yes may not realize your true feelings, since you probably hide them out of fear of rejection.

You Base Your Self-Esteem and Worth on the Basis of What You Do.

Whenever you refuse someone, you feel that your value has diminished. When you please people by saying yes, you feel better about yourself.

You Feel Indebted to the Other Person.

If you have received substantial help from someone and out of sincere gratitude you want to show your appreciation, you will be able to say yes sincerely. If you feel indebted, and therefore *obligated* to say yes, you may be feeling overpowered.

PERSONAL EVALUATION

- When have you said yes when you wanted to say no?
- Did you procrastinate when it came time to make good on your commitments?
- Considering the reasons above and other insights you have about yourself, why do you think you say yes when you wish you could say no?

ACTION

For each time you said yes when you wished you could say no, answer the following in writing: Who asked you to do something? What did they ask you to do? Why did you feel you had to say yes? What did you fear would happen if you said no?

FOOD FOR THOUGHT

Who cannot resolve upon a moment's notice to live his own life, he forever lives a slave to others.
—Gotthold Ephraim Lessing

Overwhelmed by Reality

In *Gone with the Wind,* Scarlett O'Hara repeatedly said, "I'll think about that tomorrow." Life was overwhelming, and the only way she knew to survive was to deal with as much as she could today and deal with the rest tomorrow.

Chances are slight that your world is crumbling in the way life in the southern states crumbled during the Civil War. However, you may be overwhelmed by your own reality: a failing marriage, a weighty work load, surviving financially, finishing school, grieving the death of a loved one, struggling with addictions. At times like these it is tempting to try to put off dealing with reality until you feel better able.

Here are some ways you may procrastinate when you feel overwhelmed by reality:

You May Use Mood-Altering Substances Such as Drugs and Alcohol.

Drugs or alcohol may give you a temporary respite from life. But when chemical effects wear off, your problems are still there. They may even be compounded by things you did while under the influence.

You May Use Mood-Altering Experiences.

Sex, work, eating, shopping, religion and other activities can distract you from your problems. These activities are not bad, but if they are used as an escape they can become addictive or compulsive.

You May Pretend Everything Is Fine.

Denial is a form of procrastination that buys you time by letting you believe there is nothing which needs to be done. Families living with an alcoholic may pretend there isn't a problem. You may continue writing checks until you get a notice from the bank stating that your account is overdrawn. This act of denying financial reality allows you to put off cutting back on expenses, getting a better paying job, or selling one of your cars.

PERSONAL EVALUATION

- What are you currently doing to cope with a difficult life situation?
- Are you doing anything that helps you put off dealing with reality?
- What decisions are you afraid you might be required to make in order to deal with the reality of your situation?
- Whom do you have to support you if you are in the midst of an overwhelming life situation?
- What (if any) mood altering substances or experiences do you use to help you put off having to deal with your overwhelming reality?
- What are the negative side effects from your attempts to avoid facing your true situation? What are the momentary benefits?

ACTION

If some part of your life or past is overwhelming, try to write out that which you find too much to bear. Select one person you trust as someone to confide in. Together, make a list of your fears that keep you from facing life as it really is.

REFLECTION

Acknowledging those things that threaten to overwhelm you is quite a task. Allow yourself to respect the magnitude of whatever seems so overwhelming for you, talk to your chosen confidant, and don't belittle your valid fears. If something is powerful enough to cause you to put off facing the truth, it is worthy of your respect.

If you are not overwhelmed by reality at this season of your life, reflect on your good fortune.

ENCOURAGEMENT

Even when life seems overwhelming, there is always a way through. You can find your way if you are willing to summon your courage and get help to deal with whatever life has served you.

FOOD FOR THOUGHT

You may give out, but never give up.
—Mary Crowley

Dealing with Procrastination One Day at a Time

Many people who procrastinate focus on finishing the whole project instead of completing one step at a time. For example, Vicky could step into a messy house and have it looking great in no time. Her roommate Ellen got depressed and felt overwhelmed when the house was a mess. Vicky's "secret" was that she didn't set out to clean the entire house. Instead she told herself, "I will clean the kitchen counter." Once the counter was clean, her sense of satisfaction inspired her to do other cleaning jobs. By completing a portion of the project, Vicky was able to start without being overwhelmed.

You may also take this approach to dealing with your habit of procrastination. You may procrastinate in many different ways and for different reasons, some of which are deeply rooted. If you determine to rid yourself entirely of procrastination, you will set yourself up to be intimidated by the hugeness of the assignment. *In order to be effective in kicking the habit of procrastination, you need to tackle the problem in small, manageable doses.*

If you have completed each day's journey thus far, you are already well on your way to helping yourself deal with habitual procrastination by identifying some of the things which prompt your behavior. The remainder of your journey will take each view of procrastination you have already thought about and give you simple strategies for dealing with that aspect of your behavior.

One key to your success is to *take each day's journey and do what you can* that day *to make changes to deal with your particular habit patterns.* "One day at a time" is a familiar slogan for people who use a twelve-step program to deal with addiction or other compulsive behaviors. It will be an important principle for you too.

Mark out time each day for specific tasks that help you manage time more effectively. One such practice is to review your plans for the coming day the night before. By setting aside fifteen minutes to prioritize the five or six items you plan to focus on during the coming day, you can anticipate what may need to be put off by choice rather than waiting to be caught off guard so that you end up procrastinating.

PERSONAL EVALUATION

- What projects are you currently putting off because you don't have enough time in one sitting to complete the job? How could you break the job down into smaller, more manageable portions that would not be so intimidating?
- Do you tend to see procrastination as a problem or character flaw that is too big to overcome?
- Are you willing to apply each coming day's strategy to your life?

ACTION

Focus your attention today on some project in your home that seems too big to tackle in one sitting. It may be a bookcase that needs to be reorganized or a closet that needs to be cleaned out. Think of one small part of the job you could do in less than fifteen minutes. Set a timer and work for fifteen minutes. When the limited part of the project you selected is complete or when the timer goes off, stop.

REFLECTION

Do you think that with practice you could learn to approach other projects bit by bit, rather than in large chunks? If so, how will this affect your tendency to procrastinate?

FOOD FOR THOUGHT

Take short steps. A lot of people fail because they try to take too big a step too quickly.

—Zig Ziglar

Clarifying Your Preferences and Priorities

Your priorities will change. But by clarifying what is most important to you, you can choose what to do now, what can be put off until later, and what may not be deserving of your time and attention at all. Setting up clearly defined priorities for work, family, rest and recreation allows you to accomplish what is truly important.

For example, if you were working at home and found yourself procrastinating over work while attending to household chores, you could set the following guidelines.

During work hours my priorities are:
1. Work—With projects in order of deadline and/or importance
2. Emergency needs of family members

Doing laundry, chatting with friends on the phone, or running errands would not even make your list. *If you know what your priorities are for work hours, you will find it easier to make decisions to say no to distractions.*

Your family time might be ordered in this way:
1. Make sure home is in order
2. Give attention to spouse and children
3. Welcome friends into our family

You decide what your priorities are for each part of your life. Housework should not be allowed to slip in to work time, and by clarifying the purpose of family time you could excuse yourself from even highly important work-related matters.

PERSONAL EVALUATION

- Do you have clearly defined values and priorities governing the general use of your time?
- Do you have clear priorities as to what is most important during work, family times, rest, and recreation?

ACTION

Title three sheets of paper: Priorities During Work Hours, Priorities During Family Hours, and Priorities During Rest and Recreation Hours. Under each heading write down items that are important to you. Now prioritize the items in each category.

ENCOURAGEMENT

Don't be afraid to define and clarify what is important to you in life. By having a designated time for each item, you will be more productive and experience greater peace of mind from moment to moment.

FOOD FOR THOUGHT

Establishing priorities and using your time well aren't things you can pick up at Harvard Business

School. If you want to make good use of your time, you've got to know what's important, and then give it all you've got.

—Lee Iaccoca

The Realm of What's O.K.

Some people think for every decision there is one right choice. All choices, other than the idealized "Right Choice," are wrong to varying degrees. These people look for the perfect will of God for their lives, Mr. or Ms. "Right," the perfect job, the perfect dress to wear to the ten-year reunion, and so on.

The problem with this type of viewpoint is that it makes you hesitate before making any decision, unless you are sure it is the "Right Choice." This view of life especially contributes to a procrastination habit when an individual is considering decisions that have far-reaching ramifications—such as where to attend college, which job to choose, or whom to marry.

The other problem with this point of view is that it may not be a true view of real life. I think a more realistic view of life is to look for the realm of what is O.K. In other words, be open to several acceptable possibilities. For example, in choosing a college you could look at location, areas of studies, class size, and tuition to narrow the field to several acceptable choices—your realm of that which is O.K. In areas of moral conduct, you might use the Ten Commandments as your boundaries which would tell you whether a particular decision was in the realm of what was O.K.

When you learn to view life as holding a multitude of choices, all of which are O.K. within specified boundaries, you are much more free to make decisions.

PERSONAL EVALUATION

- Do you often hesitate to make important decisions for fear that you may not make the "Right Choice"?
- Once you make a decision, are you haunted by the nagging thought that perhaps any problems you encounter are the result of not having made the "Right Choice"?
- How does your view of decision making relate to your tendency to procrastinate?
- Are you willing to consider trying a point of view which creates a realm of that which is O.K.?

ACTION

Identify one decision you are trying to make where you are concerned about making the "Right Choice."

Think about your preferences, moral boundaries, and values, then use them to help you define what possibilities can fit in the realm of what is O.K. for you.

Now that you have a wide range of options, list at least five that would be O.K. decisions.

REFLECTION

How do your feelings change about making a decision when you allow yourself to choose anything within the realm of that which is O.K. rather than demanding a perfect decision?

ENCOURAGEMENT

In a perfect world, you might be able to make perfect decisions. We don't live in a perfect world yet, so give yourself the freedom to make decisions in the realm of what is O.K.

Giving Yourself Time for Nourishment

When you make demands on yourself that do not allow time for self-nourishment, fun, and recreation, you begin experiencing what is commonly known as burn-out. In a state of walking exhaustion, you are more inclined to procrastinate because your body, mind and spirit are all telling you that you deserve a break. *If you do not choose to give yourself the things you need,* including rest, nourishment, and recreation, *you will find ways to make it up to yourself.*

Alcoholics Anonymous understands the power of deprivation. The group has a saying that reminds people to take care of their needs. The letters HALT remind members to guard against allowing themselves to become too Hungry, Angry, Lonely, or Tired. When people become deprived or undernourished, they will more likely give in to an immediate fix in order to feel better. This principle can also apply to procrastination. If you feel like you will never have any time to rest, relax, and play, you will put off work and other commitments at times when you feel like you have to have a break.

If you plan a schedule that allows you to nourish your body, mind, and spirit, you won't have to interrupt work with procrastination in order to meet your needs.

PERSONAL EVALUATION

- What do you need to do on a regular basis to nourish yourself in each of these areas: physically, intellectually, emotionally, spiritually, relationally?
- In which of these areas do you feel deprived?
- What is something you could do that would alleviate your feelings of deprivation?

ACTION

Set aside one hour each day for the express purpose of nourishing yourself in the ways that are healthiest for your own well-being. If you have not done so already, write these hours on your calendar.

Set aside one day each week when you determine not to do any work. Spend this day resting, refreshing yourself, and renewing your relationship with God.

REFLECTION

Consider how well you are able to deal with distractions when you are well nourished, as compared to when you are feeling deprived.

ENCOURAGEMENT

When you take time to nourish yourself, you will find that you are better able to resist the temptation to procrastinate when it is time to work.

FOOD FOR THOUGHT

Man is wholly himself only when he plays.
—F. Schiller

Finding Other Ways Through the Pain

Pain is always unpleasant. You will probably continue to have a normal desire to avoid pain whenever possible. However, you can help yourself get over procrastinating by recognizing the purpose pain serves and finding another way to make the pain manageable.

Some of the painful issues which cause you to procrastinate are emotional in nature. You put off dealing with particular issues that may hurt your feelings or stir up emotions which seem overwhelming. You can overcome procrastination in these situations by recognizing that there is something at the source of the painful area you are avoiding. (An example would be the memory of suppressed childhood abuse or trauma.) If an emotional issue is causing you to detour around particular people or issues, there is a good reason to deal with the pain—even if getting close to the source of the pain may hurt more for the moment. The pain is an indicator that something inside is injured and needs attention.

Some things which may cause you to procrastinate for fear of being hurt are purely physical—such as putting off a necessary visit to the dentist. If you put off going to the dentist long enough, the minor pain of a toothache can become overwhelming pain. At that point, your nerve endings are sending you a clear message that a problem needs attention. When the physical pain of not going to the dentist exceeds your fear, you will stop procrastinating. However, if you believe that seeing the dentist regularly will protect you from the excruciating pain of a toothache, you will be less inclined to procrastinate.

You will also be better able to overcome procrastination if you draw on resources which will help you deal with the pain. For example, if you are afraid of being overwhelmed by emotional pain related to dealing with childhood abuse, it may help you to talk to a counselor or to attend a support group. If you are afraid of the dentist, it will help you to know that nitrous oxide (commonly known as laughing gas) makes the pain more manageable.

PERSONAL EVALUATION

· What reason do you have to believe that facing the pain that triggers procrastination would be for your ultimate good? What relief could you find?
· What are some resources available to make your pain more manageable?

ACTION

List the things you put off because of fear over potential physical pain. Make another list of things you put off because they are associated with potential emotional pain.

For each item, ask yourself what the pain indicates. If you're not sure why you avoid some things, draw a large question mark over that item.

Identify someone as your encourager and ask him or her to help you face the areas of pain where you suspect the underlying cause.

Consider discussing the issues which you avoid, but you are not sure why, with a qualified counselor or therapist. If you are hindered in life by something you cannot identify, a counselor may be able to help you identify and resolve the problem.

REFLECTION

Imagine the sense of relief you could feel once the pain you are procrastinating over is a thing of the past and you are feeling fine again.

ENCOURAGEMENT

Dare to face the pain. When you do, you will be able to move on with your life in a much healthier way.

FOOD FOR THOUGHT

The only way out is through.
                    —Alcoholics Anonymous Slogan

Making Friends with Failure

You can learn to live on friendly terms with failure.
But you will probably have to change your understanding of what failure means. Many people who
procrastinate out of a fear of failure have been
taught that failure in one aspect of life means failure at life.

You may have learned at an early age that failure
of any kind was totally unacceptable. You quickly
learned to cover up your failures and pretend they
never occurred. If this is what you have been taught
to believe about failure, you will need to reeducate
yourself.

*The fear of failure can actually hold you
back from success.* Many people who are renowned for being the best in their respective fields
were often the biggest failures in their fields at
times. They were able to excel because they were
willing to try and fail so many times.

Here are a few examples of people who succeeded
by making friends with failure:

A young reporter had heard that Thomas Edison
had failed over ten thousand times in his attempts
to invent the light bulb. The reporter posed the
question, "Mr. Edison, how does it feel to have
failed so many times in one pursuit?" Thomas Edison replied, "My young man, I have not failed ten

thousand times. I have successfully found ten thousand ways that will not work." The fact that you are probably reading this book by the light of an incandescent bulb serves to illustrate the point that making friends with failure can lead to great success.

Babe Ruth held the world's record for the most home runs scored in professional baseball. But he also held another record. He had struck out at bat more times than any other professional ball player on record. By playing hard, Babe Ruth accepted the strikes along with the hits.

History is full of other examples of great men and women who were able to accept failure as their companion—even their friend—while on their way to greatness.

Failure can give you an opportunity to develop your sense of humor. If you are able to laugh at yourself, you will enjoy life more. You will also find that you are more fun to be around.

Failure can be your teacher. As with Thomas Edison, failure is a means of gaining valuable knowledge of what will *not* work. By knowing clearly what doesn't work for you, you will more easily find those things which do work for you.

Failure can encourage you to practice and refine. When you recognize that anyone who has learned to excel in any arena has practiced diligently, you will be more accepting of your perceived failures.

PERSONAL EVALUATION

- Were you raised to believe failure is a friend or a foe?
- How do you feel about yourself when you fail?
- Are you willing to reach out your hand in friendship to failure in your life?

ACTION

Identify an area where you are afraid to try because you are afraid to fail.

How could failure redirect your course? Develop your sense of humor? Teach you something? Encourage you to practice your craft?

REFLECTION

Babe Ruth held the record for strikes as well as for home runs. What kind of attitude allowed him to swing with all his might? How would having a similar attitude toward the possibility of failure in your life allow you to overcome procrastination?

ENCOURAGEMENT

You can make friends with failure. It may take a season of reeducating yourself, but your time and effort in this regard may result in assuring your ultimate success.

FOOD FOR THOUGHT

The Creed of the Champion

I am not judged by the number of times I fail but by the number of times I succeed, and the number of times I succeed is in direct proportion to the number of times I can fail and keep on trying.

—Tom Hopkins

Finding Your Success Comfort Zone

If you desire a brighter future that is markedly different from your past, but procrastinate out of fear of change, you must find your success comfort zone. You do this by becoming familiar with success so it becomes less threatening.

Here are some ways to create a positive attitude toward success and create a success comfort zone:

- Educate yourself about what life is really like for those who have succeeded in ways you are afraid to succeed.
- Associate with successful people. If possible join groups or make friends with people who are successful. Part of your fear of success may be that your friends might reject you if you succeed far beyond their accomplishments. *If you develop friendships with people who are more successful than you are, you create your own positive peer pressure.*
- Find mentors you want to emulate, especially if you can identify someone who has a similar background to yours but who is now *enjoying* success.
- Read books about real people who have succeeded.
- Overcome your own objections. You have already identified what you fear may happen if you were

to succeed. Review those objections and think of positive consequences of success.

PERSONAL EVALUATION

- What are you willing to do to find your success comfort zone?
- Do you have any objections to becoming successful which you find impossible to overcome? If so, are you willing to talk the matter over with someone else who may be able to help you overcome your fear of success?

ACTION

Do something to educate yourself on the rewards of success. I highly recommend the tape series by Zig Ziglar: Success and the Self-Image. The tapes are available through direct mail from the Zig Ziglar Corporation at (214) 233-9191. You may also choose to read *Living A Beautiful Life* and *Living Beautifully Together* by Alexandra Stottard. These two books are detailed guides to self-pampering and gracious living. They will help you envision the up side of success.

REFLECTION

Give yourself thirty minutes to daydream or imagine in glorious detail how your life and the lives of your loved ones could be if you were to stop procrastinating and allow yourself to be as successful as you can possibly be.

FOOD FOR THOUGHT

The important thing is this: to be able at any moment to sacrifice what we are for what we could become.

—Charles Du Bos

Finding Freedom from Shame

If you procrastinate in order to keep others from discovering how deeply flawed you feel as a human being, you may be dealing with unhealthy shame. From earlier in your journey, you realize that there is a distinction between wanting to avoid embarrassment and feeling ashamed of who you are as a person.

If you are dealing with unhealthy shame, there is no immediate solution. However, there is good help available. You will need to seek an understanding friend and perhaps the assistance of a professional therapist who can support your efforts to face parts of your life which are tremendously intimidating.

There are two books which I recommend: *Healing the Shame that Binds You* by John Bradshaw and *Your 30-Day Journey to Freedom from Shame* by C.W. Neal.

Here are some things you can do to help yourself find freedom from shame:

- Identify the sources of your shame.
- Identify resources to help you deal with shame.
- Establish a network of support.
- Find someone to whom you can safely tell your secrets.
- Limit the influence of people who shame you.
- Draw close to people who cover your shame.

- Avoid the influence of negative religion which tears you down without demonstrating God's acceptance, love, and grace.
- Acquire knowledge and skills which would help you fit in socially.
- Develop your unique talents and abilities.
- Find fulfillment in your work as much as possible.
- *Practice treating yourself with respect.*
- Find a counselor qualified to deal with the roots of shame.

PERSONAL EVALUATION

- Do you suspect that your tendency to procrastinate is associated with unhealthy shame-related issues?
- If so, are you willing to take steps to get help dealing with the root issues, rather than just trying to eliminate the symptom of procrastination?

ACTION

Get the books recommended above, and do some more reading to help you learn to deal with shame-related issues.

If possible, seek the help of a qualified counselor who deals with shame-related issues or attend an appropriate support group.

REFLECTION

How might your desire to overcome procrastination help you find relief from deeper issues? If you do not struggle with unhealthy shame, take a moment to feel a sense of gratitude to whoever raised you to know that you are a valuable human being just because you are you.

Making Your Monsters Manageable

If you procrastinate because you don't know how much something will cost, how long it will take, who can do it for you, how to go about doing it, or what needs to be done, the solution is knowledge. However, seeking knowledge can cause you to procrastinate if you are embarrassed that you don't already know the information.

Here are some resources that can help you seek knowledge you do not have:

Gain the Information Anonymously.

A telephone call may spare you the embarrassment of having to admit a lack of knowledge face-to-face.

Another way to gain knowledge anonymously is to check at your local library for books on the topic. Look in the card catalog (a file of cards that represents every book available through the library). The cards are listed by topic and by author's last name. Ask a librarian to recommend some books or guide you to the section of the library that holds the books you need.

You can also contact organizations that are set up to deal with issues related to your area of interest. A great resource for any family-related issue is Focus On The Family. The telephone number is: (719) 531-3400.

Use Your Telephone Directory.

Look under city, county, state, and federal government for numbers of agencies. If you are not sure that a particular agency can help you, call and explain what information or help you are trying to locate. Staff persons will usually know where to direct you if they cannot help you.

Check with Treatment Centers and Recovery Groups.

You can contact counseling offices, treatment centers, or universities to get leads about people, groups, and organizations that help individuals in specific ways.

Call Radio Talk Shows That Deal with Issues Related to Your Area of Interest.

Radio talk programs have to keep an extensive listing of guests who address various topics. They will probably have a list of referrals to groups and organizations as well.

Join Community Groups.

Within your community there are church groups, men's groups, women's groups, recovery groups, parenting groups, professional associations, and educational seminars. To tap into these meetings, contact your local Chamber of Commerce.

The real key to finding information and resources is to keep on seeking, keep on asking, and keep on knocking. Once you know what information or help you lack, it's just a matter of persistent effort to track down the resources.

PERSONAL EVALUATION

- Choose one thing you have procrastinated over because of something unknown.
- Identify three things you can do today to begin tracking down the kind of information you need to move past procrastination.

ACTION

Do those three things!

REFLECTION

Think about the relief you will feel and the confidence you could gain by venturing out into the unknown and overcoming whatever has kept you from doing the things you need to do.

ENCOURAGEMENT

Dare to venture out into the realm of that which you don't yet know. It's rarely as bad as you feared it would be.

FOOD FOR THOUGHT

You do not have because you do not ask.
—James 4:2

Establishing Your Personal Boundaries

Establishing personal boundaries in how you use your time can help you kick the procrastination habit.

I recently saw this humorous notice posted in a place of business. This serves as an example of how inadequate boundaries in the use of time can result in feeling like you are procrastinating.

Business Hours

OPEN Most Days about 9 or 10 Occasionally as early as 7, But SOME DAYS As Late As 12 or 1. WE CLOSE About 5:30 or 6 Occasionally About 4 or 5, But Sometimes as Late as 11 or 12. SOME DAYS OR Afternoons, We Aren't Here At All, and Lately I've Been Here Just About All The Time, Except When I'm Someplace Else, But I Should Be Here Then Too.

When the proprietor failed to establish time boundaries, she set herself up to feel as though she is putting off work she should be doing. If you give yourself clearly defined boundaries for the use of your time, you will free yourself from the feeling that you should probably be doing something else.

Setting boundaries on the use of your time will help you find relief from the pressure of procrastination in several ways. For instance, you can draw the line between time for work and time for play. When it is time to play, you will know that you are not procrastinating on work.

You can also set aside a manageable portion of time for tasks that seem overwhelming. Instead of putting off a large task until you have a major block of time to complete it, mark out thirty minutes to be spent on the task on specific days until the task is completed.

When you schedule specific blocks of time, you reduce interruptions. If someone suggests dropping by at around three and you have a set schedule to work until five, you can simply say you are not available until five. When you post scheduled activities you help others know when you are available to give them your full attention. Plus, you help yourself by cutting down on unexpected distractions.

Another benefit of scheduling is that you will not be shuffling details around. You may already schedule time for the important parts of your life such as work, school, church, and family time. But you may not schedule time for the routine duties such as paying bills, balancing your checking account, shopping, and running errands. If you give yourself time each week for the minor tasks, you won't be as likely to put them off.

PERSONAL EVALUATION

- Which tasks are you putting off until you have a large block of time to complete the entire job? Which of these tasks could be done in several smaller segments of time?

- What minor details in your life do you put off regularly? Do you set aside adequate time to do them? Are you unwilling to schedule time for these tasks because you are not willing to accept responsibility for them?

ACTION

Put your intended schedule in writing, filling in the intended purpose set aside for each block of time. Be sure that when you are finished you can clearly state the following:

- Work hours
- Time for play and relaxation each day
- Weekly day of rest
- Time for minor tasks

After your schedule is clearly defined, choose one project you have put off because it will be time-consuming. Schedule fifteen minutes three times per week to work on the project. Make sure to set a timer and only work for the set time.

REFLECTION

Think about how clarifying your personal time boundaries and communicating them to others can keep you from feeling like you are always procrastinating.

FOOD FOR THOUGHT

When you do the things you ought to do, when you ought to do them, the time will come when you can do the things you want to do, when you want to do them.

—Zig Ziglar

Making Amends

Your life is intertwined with the lives of others. *Any time you procrastinate, other people will be affected in some way.* You may cause them a minor inconvenience, or a great amount of trouble because of your failure to do things in a timely manner.

You may have seen procrastination as a personal problem which affected only your life. But it is important for you to accept responsibility for the way your behavior inconveniences or hurts others. Here is how you can accept responsibility for the results of your behavior and make amends:

1. Consider each area of activity where you have procrastinated in the past. For each part of your life, (work, school, family, friendships, and so on) consider those people whose lives touch yours, and identify how your procrastination has affected them.

2. Admit to yourself that, even though you are not purposely inconveniencing others, your lack of action may have negative consequences in others' lives.

3. Acknowledge any regret you feel over how your procrastination habit has negatively affected others. Communicate your regrets to those who have been negatively affected. For example, say, "I'm sorry I am late. I'm having a problem with

time management and am sincerely sorry for any inconvenience this caused you." If you feel uncomfortable saying this directly, send your regrets in a note.
4. Whenever possible, make amends to correct any problems you have caused. For example, if the mail in your office doesn't get out on time because you procrastinated, make amends by going out of your way to drive to the post office. That way you take the consequences rather than making others pay the price for the effects of your behavior.

ACTION

List all the people you can think of who have been negatively affected or inconvenienced by the consequences of your procrastination.

Acknowledge to them any regret you feel for having caused them inconvenience because of your problem with procrastination.

Make amends whenever possible, except when to do so would cause further problems for others.

REFLECTION

Consider how accepting responsibility for your behavior can help you in your relationships at home, work, school, and with friends.

ENCOURAGEMENT

Be willing to make amends. It will make you feel better about yourself and will improve your relationships.

The Occasional Privilege of Procrastination

There are occasions in life when you will find it is your privilege to procrastinate. To whatever degree you experience freedom in your life, *you can enjoy the freedom to procrastinate if you so choose.* Of course, your choice to procrastinate will require that you are also willing to pay the price. For example, you can delay returning library books on the due date if you prefer, as long as you are willing to pay the fines.

The human body itself teaches us that there are times when the privilege of procrastination can be in your best interest. Whenever the human system is traumatized, the body and mind may go into shock to protect the person. Shock is the body and mind's way of putting off the full physical and emotional impact of overwhelming events until the person will be better able to deal with them. At times in your life when you are hit with any sudden trauma, it is your privilege to procrastinate until you are able to absorb what has happened and respond appropriately.

There are other times when using the privilege of procrastination can benefit you. In bargaining and negotiating sessions, taking your time before taking action or revealing your full intentions can be to great advantage. In cases like this, procrastination may be a fine art.

Sometimes, having the privilege of being able to take your time shows that you are not in desperate straits. People who are at the ends of their ropes don't have the privilege of taking their time to make decisions about various options for their lives. For example, if you are seeking employment and have used the last of your savings, you may be forced to take whatever job is offered. Your financial limitations don't afford you the privilege of waiting for the job you prefer.

There are times when you should not choose to procrastinate because to do so inconveniences others.

PERSONAL EVALUATION

- Can you take comfort in realizing that you will not have to give up procrastinating entirely?
- Do you accept that it is not your right or privilege to procrastinate if to do so violates a commitment you made or hurts others?

ACTION

If there is something you can procrastinate over without hurting or inconveniencing others, weigh the cost involved and decide if you want to use the privilege of procrastination.

REFLECTION

How do you feel knowing that you can still procrastinate without having to do so compulsively or habitually?

Progressing on the Deferred Payment Plan

Kicking the procrastination habit can seem like a major project. But your goal is not unreachable, you merely need to give yourself some time. Simply approach the problem in the familiar way most Americans purchase a home or a car: Use the installment plan. By using an installment plan you: calculate and negotiate the cost; clearly define your commitment; break the payments down into amounts you can afford; spread the payments out over a manageable span of time; and make a personal commitment. When the commitment is sealed, you begin to live in the house or drive the car—even though ownership is not yet completed.

You can use the same method to kick the procrastination habit. Figure out your options; break the problem down into manageable areas; spread your recovery plans out over the course of moments, days, weeks, months, and years to come.

Carefully consider what you need to deal with in order to live your life freely, weigh your decision within the realm of what is O.K., define precisely what you are committing yourself to do, then *begin to live your life in new ways, one day at a time.* Begin to live according to the priorities you have chosen. Rely on the support system you arrange. Continue to make "payments" (taking the actions you have committed yourself to) on a schedule. You would also do well to have someone to whom you're accountable to continue making these "payments" or habit changes.

PERSONAL EVALUATION

- Are you willing to set aside a small amount of time each day to review your life and commitments and to think about doing the things you find helpful in kicking the procrastination habit?
- Are you willing to make a long-term commitment to deal with the issues you have discovered during this journey?
- Are you willing to allow someone you trust to encourage you and hold you accountable to continue making the payments necessary to live free of chronic procrastination?

ACTION

Reserve time in your schedule to continue making investments in your recovery from a life-style of habitual procrastination.

Write out a few ways you aim to change your life-style and thought patterns to help you keep from habitually procrastinating.

Discuss these changes you want to make with someone you trust. Allow this person to encourage you and to hold you accountable to continue living in ways that help you kick the procrastination habit.

REFLECTION

It has been said that time heals all wounds. This is not true! Time alone does not heal any injury, or solve any problem. But your choice to give yourself some time to tend your wounds and nourish yourself is a very important choice. Consider how learning to kick the procrastination habit will help make time a healing agent rather than your enemy.

FOOD FOR THOUGHT

What wound did ever heal but by degrees?
—William Shakespeare

Evaluate and Celebrate Your Progress

Although you have come to the end of the 30-day journey outlined in this book, your personal journey continues. I hope you have come to recognize that you *can* kick the procrastination habit. You have the freedom and the ability to understand why you tend to put things off and to choose alternatives which are beneficial to you. You even have the freedom to choose times when procrastination is a good way for you to accomplish your purpose. You will still have to practice new ways of life in order to stay free of habitual procrastination, but you can change your life.

You may underestimate the value of what you have done during this journey. *You deserve to be commended for the time, consideration, effort, and self-evaluation you have devoted to this journey.* Be sure to give yourself credit for what you have done. Discuss your journey with others. Do something to celebrate the completion of your journey, regardless of how long it took for you to complete it.

During this 30-day journey, you may have discovered that your tendency to procrastinate is a symptom of deeper issues which need attention. If you find your tendency to procrastinate is compulsive, or beyond your reasonable efforts to manage, get some professional help to discover and resolve the underlying causes for your hesitation.

The important thing is not to lose momentum. Each day, one day at a time, keep your dreams clearly in sight, your goals well defined, your tasks identified, your obstacles targeted for attack, and your relationships growing. The journey continues. Don't let a baffling battle with procrastination rob you of a full and rewarding life.

PERSONAL EVALUATION

- What have you learned to put off by choice?
- What have you learned about yourself that helps you put off the feeling that you should be doing something else?
- What issues that prompt you to procrastinate have you identified as needing further attention?

ACTION

List the things you have learned about yourself as the result of taking this journey.

List the life changes you have made as a result of taking this journey.

List the areas of interest you have discovered. Include a list of books, tapes, and other resources you plan to explore.

REFLECTION

How do you feel different about yourself and your life-style now that you have completed this journey?

ENCOURAGEMENT

Your completion of this journey is evidence that you can overcome procrastination to accomplish those things which you value. I wish you all the best as you become more fully able to live your life to the utmost.

FOOD FOR THOUGHT

We cannot do everything at once, but we can do something at once.

—Calvin Coolidge

Appendix
A Checklist for Kicking the Procrastination Habit

DAY 1: You Don't Have to Do This!

I procrastinate over things that

- ☐ feel like obligations
- ☐ may be inconsistent with my values
- ☐ may be less important than other things I need to do
- ☐ make me fear failure

After considering my motives

- ☐ I choose to take this journey
- ☐ I choose not to take this journey

DAY 2: Procrastination Serves Your Purposes

Procrastination

- ☐ helps me sort out what is important to me
- ☐ helps me avoid issues and situations that could prove painful, embarrassing, shameful, or difficult
- ☐ allows me to avoid coming face-to-face with my human flaws
- ☐ helps me remain in the comfort of the familiar

☐ is a useful way of communicating feelings that I would never put into words

☐ is a way of gaining power over someone in a position of power over me

☐ allows me to get out of doing things I don't want to do

☐ provides me with a buffer between myself and discovering the best of my ability

☐ allows me to make promises with the chance of not having to follow through

☐ keeps me from being overwhelmed

☐ keeps me from making a wrong decision by making no decision

☐ gives me enjoyment I feel I am being deprived of in my daily commitments

☐ protects me from facing activities and situations that trigger unresolved emotional issues

☐ gives me a high feeling when I put things off then rush to achieve whatever is required

---

DAY 3: Kicking the Habit Means Learning to Choose

To kick my procrastination habit, I must choose to

☐ expect less of myself in a given time frame

☐ decide how I want to live my life

☐ trade, delegate, and dump some duties

☐ hire someone to do the things I
keep putting off
☐ redefine my commitments more
realistically
☐ lower the stakes

DAY 4: Finding Motivation, Envisioning Your Rewards

The areas of my life
that would be most
improved by
kicking my
procrastination habit
are

☐ career
☐ family
☐ finances
☐ personal

☐ emotional
☐ spiritual
☐ friendships
☐ health

DAY 5: Give Yourself Some Slack

To give myself
some slack, I
need to

☐ consider whether perfectionism
is an issue I need to redefine
☐ understand and accept my
personality and personal style
☐ understand and accept my
internal time clock

DAY 6: Neglect, Avoidance, or Refusal?

The reason(s) I
procrastinate is
(are)

☐ neglect of things I should do
☐ avoidance of things that stir up
unpleasant emotions
☐ refusal to accept responsibility

DAY 7: Minor Details: It Is Just Not That Important!

To simplify my life, it is important that I

- ☐ identify what is of minor importance in this season of my life
- ☐ take obligations off my mental list
- ☐ find more efficient ways to accomplish things that are important or necessary parts of life
- ☐ get rid of possessions that require too much upkeep

DAY 8: Confused or Conflicting Priorities

Areas where I procrastinate because of confused or conflicting priorities

- ☐ family relationships
- ☐ marriage
- ☐ cultivating friendships
- ☐ dating
- ☐ parenting
- ☐ work
- ☐ hobbies
- ☐ political involvement
- ☐ civic involvement
- ☐ education
- ☐ recreation
- ☐ spirituality
- ☐ physical fitness
- ☐ creating and managing home

DAY 9: Time Out: Overcommitted and Undernourished

Areas of my life where I feel undernourished are ☐ physical ☐ emotional ☐ mental ☐ spiritual

DAY 10: Please . . . No Pain

I suspect that I sometimes procrastinate to avoid pain ☐ yes ☐ no

I procrastinate over some things but can identify only a vague uneasiness or irrational resistance ☐ yes ☐ no

I am certain that I procrastinate over some things to avoid pain but cannot identify the pain I'm avoiding at this point ☐ yes ☐ no

I am certain that I procrastinate over some things to avoid pain and can identify the pain I'm avoiding ☐ yes ☐ no

125

> ## DAY 11: Avoiding Embarrassment and Shame

I procrastinate over
some things to avoid
embarrassment

☐ yes   ☐ no

I procrastinate over
some things to avoid
shame

☐ yes   ☐ no

> ## DAY 12: Fear of Failure, Fear of Success

I procrastinate over
some things because
of fear of failure

☐ yes   ☐ no

Risks I associate
with the
possibility of
failure are

☐ damage to my self-esteem

☐ being judged by others who have
   power over my quality of life
☐ revealing how I compare to
   someone's ideal

I procrastinate over
some things because
of fear of success

☐ yes   ☐ no

Risks I associate
with the
possibility of
success are

☐ resentment of others
☐ insincerity by those who claim
   to love me or care about me
☐ higher expectations at work to
   the point of becoming
   overwhelmed
☐ life-style changes

DAY 13: Monsters in the Dark: Fear of the Unknown

I procrastinate over
some things because
the unknown
intimidates me   ☐ yes   ☐ no

DAY 14: The Silent Power of Procrastination

I sometimes
procrastinate to give
myself a sense of
power   ☐ yes   ☐ no

I sometimes
procrastinate to
convey a message or
an emotional
statement that I am
unwilling to state
verbally   ☐ yes   ☐ no

Procrastinating to
show power has
backfired on me in
the past   ☐ yes   ☐ no

DAY 15: Promising to Please: Thinking "No" but Saying "Yes"

Reasons I say
yes when I want
to say no are   ☐ I fear others' reactions
                ☐ I feel it is part of my role to say
                  yes

127

☐ I want to be seen in a positive light
☐ I fear rejection
☐ I base my self-esteem and worth on what I do
☐ I feel indebted to others

DAY 16: Overwhelmed by Reality

I procrastinate when I feel overwhelmed by reality by

☐ using mood-altering substances
☐ using mood-altering experiences
☐ pretending everything is fine

DAY 17: Dealing with Procrastination One Day at a Time

There is at least one project I'm procrastinating over because it's too big to complete in one sitting

☐ yes   ☐ no

I have thought of one part of the project that I can do in fifteen minutes

☐ yes   ☐ no

DAY 18: Clarifying Your Preferences and Priorities

The area where
my priorities
most need
defining is

☐ work hours
☐ family hours
☐ rest and recreation hours

DAY 19: The Realm of What's O.K.

I sometimes
procrastinate because
I want to make the
"Right Choice"

☐ yes   ☐ no

Areas where I
procrastinate
because I want
to make the
"Right Choice"
about a major
decision include

☐ education
☐ vocation
☐ marriage

DAY 20: Giving Yourself Time for Nourishment

I tend to procrastinate
most when I am

☐ hungry   ☐ lonely
☐ angry   ☐ tired

The area where I
most need
nourishment is

☐ physical   ☐ spiritual
☐ intellectual   ☐ relational
☐ emotional

DAY 21: Finding Other Ways Through the Pain

The pain I avoid   ☐ physical
by procrastinating   ☐ emotional
is largely

There are some areas   ☐ yes   ☐ no
of pain I need to
discuss with an
encourager

There are some issues   ☐ yes   ☐ no
I need to discuss with
a counselor or
therapist

DAY 22: Making Friends with Failure

I was raised to believe   ☐ yes   ☐ no
failure is a foe

I can most   ☐ an opportunity to develop my
readily accept   sense of humor
failure as   ☐ a teacher
                     ☐ an encouragement to practice
                       and refine

DAY 23: Finding Your Success Comfort Zone

Steps I need to   ☐ educate myself about what life
take to develop   is like for those who have
my success   succeeded
comfort zone are   ☐ associate with successful people
                     ☐ find mentors to emulate

☐ read books about people who
have succeeded

☐ overcome my own objections

DAY 24: Finding Freedom from Shame

Steps I will take
to find freedom
from shame
are

☐ identify the sources of my shame
☐ identify resources to help me
deal with shame
☐ establish a network of support
☐ find someone to whom I can
safely tell my secrets
☐ limit the influence of people who
shame me
☐ draw close to people who cover
my shame
☐ avoid the influence of negative
religion
☐ acquire knowledge and skills that
will help me fit in socially
☐ develop my talents and abilities
☐ find fulfillment in my work
☐ practice treating myself with
respect
☐ find a counselor qualified to deal
with the roots of shame

| DAY 25: Making Your Monsters Manageable |

Resources I plan
to use to get
the knowledge I
need to move
past
procrastination

☐ library
☐ organizations dealing with
  issues I'm interested in
☐ telephone directory
☐ treatment centers and recovery
  groups
☐ radio talk shows that deal with
  issues I'm interested in
☐ community groups

| DAY 26: Establishing Your Personal Boundaries |

Setting
boundaries on
the use of my
time will relieve
the pressure of
procrastination

☐ designating time for play as
  well as work
☐ setting aside manageable
  portions of time for tasks that
  seem overwhelming
☐ reducing interruptions and
  distractions
☐ allowing time for giving others
  my full attention
☐ making detail shuffling
  unnecessary

| DAY 27: Making Amends |

I need to make
amends to

☐ family members
☐ people at work
☐ people at school
☐ friends

DAY 28: The Occasional Privilege of Procrastination

I will probably
exercise the
occasional
privilege of
procrastination

☐ at home   ☐ at school
☐ at work   ☐ with friends

DAY 29: Progressing on the Deferred Payment Plan

Steps I'm
willing to take
to kick the
procrastination
habit are

☐ set aside time each day to make
   "investments" in changing my
   life-style
☐ make a long-term commitment
   to deal with the issues I've
   discovered
☐ allow someone I trust to
   encourage me and hold me
   accountable

DAY 30: Evaluate and Celebrate Your Progress

I will continue
my progress by

☐ giving myself credit and
   celebrating
☐ discussing my journey with
   others
☐ getting professional help to
   discover and resolve underlying
   issues

Sometimes problems are too difficult to handle alone on a 30-day journey. If you feel that you need additional help, please talk with one of the counselors at New Life Treatment Centers. The call is confidential and free.

1-800-NEW-LIFE